KT-160-503

# KEEP CALM AT CHRISTMAS

*For Esme, Clara and Toby,*
*who love Christmas*

# KEEP CALM AT CHRISTMAS

## GOOD ADVICE FOR CHRISTMAS TIME

EBURY PRESS

3 5 7 9 10 8 6 4

This edition published 2011
First published in 2011 by Ebury Press, an imprint of Ebury Publishing
A Random House Group company

Copyright © Ebury Press 2011

All rights reserved. No part of this publication may be reproduced, stored in a retrieval system, or transmitted in any form or by any means, electronic, mechanical, photocopying, recording or otherwise, without the prior permission of the copyright owner

The Random House Group Limited Reg. No. 954009

Addresses for companies within the Random House Group can be found at www.randomhouse.co.uk

A CIP catalogue record for this book is available from the British Library

The Random House Group Limited supports The Forest Stewardship Council (FSC®), the leading international forest certification organisation. Our books carrying the FSC label are printed on FSC® certified paper. FSC is the only forest certification scheme endorsed by the leading environmental organisations, including Greenpeace. Our paper procurement policy can be found at www.randomhouse.co.uk/environment

FSC
www.fsc.org
MIX
Paper from responsible sources
FSC® C016897

Designed and set by seagulls.net

Printed in Germany by GGP Media GmbH, Pössneck

ISBN 9780091945053

To buy books by your favourite authors and register for offers visit www.randomhouse.co.uk

**A CHRISTMAS GAMBOL OFT COULD CHEER THE POOR MAN'S HEART THROUGH HALF THE YEAR.**

*Sir Walter Scott*

# CONTENTS

Introduction

Christmas
Holidays
Parties
Shopping
Expense
Home for Christmas
Deck the Halls
Snow
Christmas Eve
Santa

The giving…

…And the receiving of gifts

Children

Friends and family

The turkey

Food

Drink

Overindulgence

Christmas TV

Goodwill to all men

Bah humbug

Comfort and joy

Religion

Spirit of Christmas

New Year

# INTRODUCTION

Christmas comes but once a year, goes the old saying – even if it does now appear to begin in late September and carry on into the first weeks of the New Year. This early arrival and late departure, driven by the financial concerns of greedy merchants, is meat and drink to certain kind of curmudgeon. Despite their protests at the deplorable commercialisation of Christmas, they take secret joy in spotting its ever-earlier arrival, probably plotting the dates on a spreadsheet and exploring the correlations between the premature arrival of tinsel in the shops and the lack of backbone in the nation's youth.

The traditional nativity scene, with the infant and mother centre stage surrounded by shepherds, wise men and lowing cattle (Joseph lurking at the back looking a bit embarrassed; turns out he's not even the real father), is still one that most of us recognise. Anyone acquainted with young children will have seen the Christmas story played out simply and movingly, often enhanced with supporting characters puzzlingly absent from the Gospels: talking mice, stable-dwelling lobsters and even Bethlehem-bound ninja turtles.

Somewhere in the tangle of Christmas lies its religious, dogmatic heart: do you follow the creed of Delia, Jamie or Gordon when it comes to cooking the turkey? Eating and drinking to excess, as demanded by convention, is a key element to a satisfactory Yule. Apart from Christmas morning, stag parties are the only other legitimate occasions when

it is considered good form to start drinking at breakfast. Gorging throughout the day before descending into a food- and alcohol-induced coma around late afternoon, from which one is roused in the time-honoured custom of an invitation to play charades, is the shape of Christmas for many.

But beneath the hype, the relentless merchandising, the fake snow and the sound of Slade echoing through every shopping centre in Britain, the magic of Christmas is still there. Why else would we put so much effort into getting it right, and be so disappointed if it flops, if deep down we didn't still have a splinter of the excitement and wonder of the Christmases of childhood in our hearts? We still all hope for the innocent pleasure of a white Christmas, just like the ones we probably never really knew. We have an image of what the perfect Christmas should be like and we cleave to the idea, even

as we slope into the bookies for a bet on whether a snowflake will fall on the Met Office roof on the 25th December.

Nonetheless, it seems that whatever we throw at Christmas, it still comes through with its old magic and promise of a respite from the daily grind, and a time to appreciate the things that really matter. Like friends, family, and the *Morecambe and Wise Christmas Special.* So use the advice of this little tome to steel yourself for the stress-inducing marathon that awaits. Keep Calm and Merry Christmas.

# CHRISTMAS

**A MERRY CHRISTMAS TO EVERYBODY! A HAPPY NEW YEAR TO ALL THE WORLD!**

*Charles Dickens*

**I HEARD THE BELLS ON CHRISTMAS DAY. THEIR OLD FAMILIAR CAROLS PLAY. AND WILD AND SWEET THE WORDS REPEAT. OF PEACE ON EARTH GOODWILL TO MEN.**

*Henry Wadsworth Longfellow*

**CHRISTMAS IS A NECESSITY. THERE HAS TO BE AT LEAST ONE DAY OF THE YEAR TO REMIND US THAT WE'RE HERE FOR SOMETHING ELSE BESIDES OURSELVES.**

*Eric Sevareid*

**IT IS CHRISTMAS IN THE HEART THAT PUTS CHRISTMAS IN THE AIR.**

*W T Ellis*

**CHRISTMAS IS THE DAY THAT HOLDS ALL TIME TOGETHER.**

*Alexander Smith*

# HOLIDAYS

IT IS THE ONE SEASON OF THE YEAR WHEN WE CAN LAY ASIDE ALL GNAWING WORRY, INDULGE IN SENTIMENT WITHOUT CENSURE, ASSUME THE CAREFREE FAITH OF CHILDHOOD, AND JUST PLAIN 'HAVE FUN.' WHETHER THEY

**CALL IT YULETIDE, NOEL, WEINACHTEN, OR CHRISTMAS, PEOPLE AROUND THE EARTH THIRST FOR ITS REFRESHMENT AS THE DESERT TRAVELLER FOR THE OASIS.**

*D D Monroe*

**I ONCE WANTED TO BECOME AN ATHEIST, BUT I GAVE UP — THEY HAVE NO HOLIDAYS.**

*Henry Youngman*

**NOTHING SAYS HOLIDAYS, LIKE A CHEESE LOG.**

*Ellen DeGeneres*

# PARTIES

**CHRISTMAS IS A TIME WHEN EVERYBODY WANTS HIS PAST FORGOTTEN AND HIS PRESENT REMEMBERED. WHAT I DON'T LIKE ABOUT OFFICE CHRISTMAS PARTIES IS LOOKING FOR A JOB THE NEXT DAY.**

*Phyllis Diller*

**AT EVERY PARTY THERE ARE TWO KINDS OF PEOPLE — THOSE WHO WANT TO GO HOME AND THOSE WHO DON'T. THE TROUBLE IS, THEY ARE USUALLY MARRIED TO EACH OTHER.**

*Ann Landers*

**HEAR NO EVIL, SPEAK NO EVIL — AND YOU'LL NEVER BE INVITED TO A PARTY.**

*Oscar Wilde*

**NEVER BE THE FIRST TO ARRIVE AT A PARTY OR THE LAST TO GO HOME, AND NEVER, EVER BE BOTH.**

*David Brown*

**A DOG IS FOR LIFE, NOT JUST FOR CHRISTMAS. SO BE CAREFUL AT THE OFFICE CHRISTMAS PARTY.**

*Jimmy Carr*

**AT THE OFFICE PARTY YOU'RE SUPPOSED TO SIT NAKED ON TOP OF THE PHOTOCOPIER, NOT THE SHREDDER.**

*David Letterman*

# NO MAN DOES RIGHT BY A WOMAN AT A PARTY.

*Harry Golden*

# SHOPPING

**FROM A COMMERCIAL POINT OF VIEW, IF CHRISTMAS DID NOT EXIST IT WOULD BE NECESSARY TO INVENT IT.**

*Katharine Whitehorn*

**TO PERCEIVE CHRISTMAS THROUGH ITS WRAPPINGS BECOMES MORE DIFFICULT WITH EVERY YEAR.**

*E B White*

**ONCE AGAIN, WE COME TO THE HOLIDAY SEASON, A DEEPLY RELIGIOUS TIME THAT EACH OF US OBSERVES, IN HIS OWN WAY, BY GOING TO THE MALL OF HIS CHOICE.**

*Dave Barry*

# IF MEN LIKED SHOPPING, THEY'D CALL IT RESEARCH.

*Cynthia Nelms*

# A CHRISTMAS SHOPPER'S COMPLAINT IS ONE OF LONG-STANDING.

*Anon*

# EXPENSE

**ABOUT ALL YOU CAN DO IS DREAM OF A WHITE CHRISTMAS, FOR IT SEEMS LIKE IT ALWAYS LEAVES MOST OF US IN THE RED.**

*Anon*

**OH, FOR THE GOOD OLD DAYS WHEN PEOPLE WOULD STOP CHRISTMAS SHOPPING WHEN THEY RAN OUT OF MONEY.**

*Anon*

**CHRISTMAS IS THE TIME WHEN KIDS TELL SANTA WHAT THEY WANT AND ADULTS PAY FOR IT. DEFICITS ARE WHEN ADULTS TELL GOVERNMENT WHAT THEY WANT AND THEIR KIDS PAY FOR IT.**

*Robert Lamm*

**THE CHRISTMAS SEASON HAS COME TO MEAN THE PERIOD WHEN THE PUBLIC PLAYS SANTA CLAUS TO THE MERCHANTS.**

*John Andrew Holmes*

**MANY BANKS HAVE A NEW KIND OF CHRISTMAS CLUB IN OPERATION. THE NEW CLUB HELPS YOU SAVE MONEY TO PAY FOR LAST YEAR'S GIFTS.**

*Anon*

# HOME FOR CHRISTMAS

**FOR CENTURIES MEN HAVE KEPT AN APPOINTMENT WITH CHRISTMAS. CHRISTMAS MEANS FELLOWSHIP, FEASTING, GIVING AND RECEIVING, A TIME OF GOOD CHEER, HOME.**

*W J Ronald Tucker*

**AT CHRISTMAS, ALL ROADS LEAD HOME.**

*Marjorie Holmes*

**HAPPY, HAPPY CHRISTMAS, THAT CAN WIN US BACK TO THE DELUSIONS OF OUR CHILDHOOD DAYS, RECALL TO THE OLD MAN THE PLEASURES OF HIS YOUTH, AND TRANSPORT THE TRAVELLER BACK TO HIS OWN FIRESIDE AND QUIET HOME!**

*Charles Dickens*

# DECK THE HALLS

**NO MATTER HOW CAREFULLY YOU STORED THE LIGHTS LAST YEAR, THEY WILL BE SNARLED AGAIN THIS CHRISTMAS.**

*Robert Kirby*

# TINSEL IS REALLY SNAKES' MIRRORS.

*Steven Wright*

**NEVER WORRY ABOUT THE SIZE OF YOUR CHRISTMAS TREE. IN THE EYES OF CHILDREN, THEY ARE ALL 30 FEET TALL.**

*Larry Wilde*

**PERHAPS THE BEST YULETIDE DECORATION IS BEING WREATHED IN SMILES.**

*Anon*

# SNOW

# A GREEN CHRISTMAS MAKES A FAT CHURCHYARD.

*English proverb*

**THE AGEING PROCESS HAS YOU FIRMLY IN ITS GRASP IF YOU NEVER GET THE URGE TO THROW A SNOWBALL.**

*Doug Larson*

**THE FIRST FALL OF SNOW IS NOT ONLY AN EVENT, IT IS A MAGICAL EVENT. YOU GO TO BED IN ONE KIND OF A WORLD AND WAKE UP IN ANOTHER QUITE DIFFERENT, AND IF THIS IS NOT ENCHANTMENT THEN WHERE IS IT TO BE FOUND?**

*J B Priestley*

**THERE'S ONE GOOD THING ABOUT SNOW, IT MAKES YOUR LAWN LOOK AS NICE AS YOUR NEIGHBOUR'S.**

*Clyde Moore*

# CHRISTMAS EVE

# THERE ARE NO STRANGERS ON CHRISTMAS EVE.

*George Melton (Harry Carey)*
*in 'Beyond Tomorow'*

**IT'S CHRISTMAS EVE. IT'S THE ONE NIGHT OF THE YEAR WHEN WE ALL ACT A LITTLE NICER, WE SMILE A LITTLE EASIER, WE CHEER A LITTLE MORE. FOR A COUPLE OF HOURS OUT OF THE WHOLE YEAR WE ARE THE PEOPLE THAT WE ALWAYS HOPED WE WOULD BE.**

*Frank Cross (Bill Murray) in 'Scrooged'*

# LET'S BE NAUGHTY AND SAVE SANTA THE TRIP.

*Gary Allen*

# SANTA

**THE MAIN REASON SANTA IS SO JOLLY IS BECAUSE HE KNOWS WHERE ALL THE BAD GIRLS LIVE.**

*George Carlin*

# YOU KNOW YOU'RE GETTING OLD, WHEN SANTA STARTS LOOKING YOUNGER.

*Robert Paul*

**WHY IS CHRISTMAS JUST LIKE A DAY AT THE OFFICE? YOU DO ALL THE WORK AND THE FAT GUY WITH THE SUIT GETS ALL THE CREDIT.**

*Anon*

**THERE ARE THREE STAGES OF MAN: HE BELIEVES IN SANTA CLAUS; HE DOES NOT BELIEVE IN SANTA CLAUS; HE IS SANTA CLAUS.**

*Bob Phillips*

**WHAT DO YOU CALL PEOPLE WHO ARE AFRAID OF SANTA CLAUS? CLAUSTROPHOBIC.**

*Anon*

# THE GIVING...

**NOTHING'S AS MEAN AS GIVING A LITTLE CHILD SOMETHING USEFUL FOR CHRISTMAS.**

*Kin Hubbard*

**WE SHOULD GIVE AS WE WOULD RECEIVE, CHEERFULLY, QUICKLY, AND WITHOUT HESITATION; FOR THERE IS NO GRACE IN A BENEFIT THAT STICKS TO THE FINGERS.**

*Seneca*

# GUILT: THE GIFT THAT KEEPS ON GIVING.

*Erma Bombeck*

**MAIL YOUR PACKAGES EARLY SO THE POST OFFICE CAN LOSE THEM IN TIME FOR CHRISTMAS.**

*Johnny Carson*

**EVERY GIFT WHICH IS GIVEN, EVEN THOUGH IT BE SMALL, IS IN REALITY GREAT, IF IT IS GIVEN WITH AFFECTION.**

*Pindar*

**ANYONE WHO BELIEVES THAT MEN ARE THE EQUAL OF WOMEN HAS NEVER SEEN A MAN TRYING TO WRAP A CHRISTMAS PRESENT.**

*Anon*

**PRESENTS ARE THE BEST WAY TO SHOW SOMEONE HOW MUCH YOU CARE. IT IS LIKE THIS TANGIBLE THING THAT YOU CAN POINT TO AND SAY 'HEY MAN, I LOVE YOU THIS MANY DOLLARS WORTH.'**

*Michael Scott (Steve Carell) in 'The Office'*

# ...AND THE RECEIVING OF GIFTS

**THE ONE THING WOMEN DON'T WANT TO FIND IN THEIR STOCKINGS ON CHRISTMAS MORNING IS THEIR HUSBAND.**

*Joan Rivers*

**IN SUGGESTING GIFTS: MONEY IS APPROPRIATE, AND ONE SIZE FITS ALL.**

*William Randolph Hearst*

**PRESENTS,
I OFTEN SAY,
ENDEAR ABSENTS.**

*Charles Lamb*

# CHILDREN

**THERE'S NOTHING SADDER IN THIS WORLD THAN TO AWAKE CHRISTMAS MORNING AND NOT BE A CHILD.**

*Erma Bombeck*

**CHRISTMAS TO A CHILD IS THE FIRST TERRIBLE PROOF THAT TO TRAVEL HOPEFULLY IS BETTER THAN TO ARRIVE.**

*Stephen Fry*

**NO SELF-RESPECTING MOTHER WOULD RUN OUT OF INTIMIDATIONS ON THE EVE OF A MAJOR HOLIDAY.**

*Erma Bombeck*

**THREE PHRASES THAT SUM UP CHRISTMAS ARE: PEACE ON EARTH, GOODWILL TO MEN, AND BATTERIES NOT INCLUDED.**

*Anon*

**A CHILD THAT'S BORN ON A CHRISTMAS DAY, IS FAIR AND WISE, GOOD AND GAY.**

*English proverb*

# FRIENDS AND FAMILY

**VISITS ALWAYS GIVE PLEASURE — IF NOT THE ARRIVAL, THE DEPARTURE.**

*Portuguese proverb*

**SANTA CLAUS HAS THE RIGHT IDEA — VISIT PEOPLE ONLY ONCE A YEAR.**

*Victor Borge*

**WHEN OUR RELATIVES ARE AT HOME, WE HAVE TO THINK OF ALL THEIR GOOD POINTS OR IT WOULD BE IMPOSSIBLE TO ENDURE THEM.**

*George Bernard Shaw*

**HAPPINESS IS HAVING A LARGE, LOVING, CARING, CLOSE-KNIT FAMILY IN ANOTHER CITY.**

*George Burns*

# FISH AND VISITORS SMELL IN THREE DAYS.

*Benjamin Franklin*

**FAMILIES ARE LIKE FUDGE — MOSTLY SWEET WITH A FEW NUTS.**

*Anon*

**IF YOU CANNOT GET RID OF THE FAMILY SKELETON, YOU MAY AS WELL MAKE IT DANCE.**

*George Bernard Shaw*

**PEOPLE REALLY ACT WEIRD AT CHRISTMAS TIME! WHAT OTHER TIME OF YEAR DO YOU SIT IN FRONT OF A DEAD TREE IN THE LIVING ROOM AND EAT NUTS AND SWEETS OUT OF YOUR SOCKS?**

*Anon*

# THE TURKEY

# A TURKEY NEVER VOTED FOR AN EARLY CHRISTMAS.

*Irish proverb*

**MOST TURKEYS TASTE BETTER THE DAY AFTER; MY MOTHER'S TASTED BETTER THE DAY BEFORE.**

*Rita Rudner*

# FOOD

**CHRISTMAS ITSELF MAY BE CALLED INTO QUESTION, IF CARRIED SO FAR IT CREATES INDIGESTION.**

*Ralph Bergengren*

**THE WORST GIFT IS A FRUITCAKE. THERE IS ONLY ONE FRUITCAKE IN THE ENTIRE WORLD, AND PEOPLE KEEP SENDING IT TO EACH OTHER.**

*Johnny Carson*

# I TRUST CHRISTMAS BRINGS TO YOU ITS TRADITIONAL MIX OF GOOD FOOD AND VIOLENT STOMACH CRAMPS.

*Ebenezer Blackadder (Rowan Atkinson) in 'Blackadder's Christmas Carol'*

**EAT AND DRINK ON CHRISTMAS — FOR EASTER, NEW CLOTHING.**

*Irish proverb*

# DRINK

**THE PROPER BEHAVIOUR ALL THROUGH THE HOLIDAY SEASON IS TO BE DRUNK. THIS DRUNKENNESS CULMINATES ON NEW YEAR'S EVE, WHEN YOU GET SO DRUNK YOU KISS THE PERSON YOU'RE MARRIED TO.**

*P J O'Rourke*

**DO NOT ALLOW CHILDREN TO MIX DRINKS. IT IS UNSEEMLY AND THEY USE TOO MUCH VERMOUTH.**

*Steve Allen*

**SOMETIMES TOO MUCH TO DRINK IS BARELY ENOUGH.**

*Mark Twain*

**THERE'S NOTHING LIKE A COLD BEER ON A HOT CHRISTMAS MORNING.**

*Homer Simpson*

# OVER-INDULGENCE

**PEOPLE ARE SO WORRIED ABOUT WHAT THEY EAT BETWEEN CHRISTMAS AND THE NEW YEAR, BUT THEY REALLY SHOULD BE WORRIED ABOUT WHAT THEY EAT BETWEEN THE NEW YEAR AND CHRISTMAS.**

*Anon*

# DYSPEPSIA IS THE REMORSE OF A GUILTY STOMACH.

*A Kerr*

**IF YOUR STOMACH DISPUTES YOU, LIE DOWN AND PACIFY IT WITH COOL THOUGHTS.**

*Satchel Paige*

# EAT, DRINK, AND BE MERRY, FOR TOMORROW YE DIET.

*William Gilmore Beymer*

# CHRISTMAS TV

OH LOOK, YET ANOTHER CHRISTMAS TV SPECIAL! HOW TOUCHING TO HAVE THE MEANING OF CHRISTMAS BROUGHT TO US BY COLA, FAST FOOD, AND BEER... WHO'D HAVE EVER

**GUESSED THAT PRODUCT CONSUMPTION, POPULAR ENTERTAINMENT, AND SPIRITUALITY WOULD MIX SO HARMONIOUSLY?**

*Calvin and Hobbes*

# IF GOD HAD MEANT CHRISTMAS TO BE A FAMILY OCCASION HE WOULDN'T HAVE INVENTED TV, WOULD HE?

*Rory McGrath*

# GOODWILL TO ALL MEN

**CHRISTMAS IS THE SEASON FOR KINDLING THE FIRE OF HOSPITALITY IN THE HALL, THE GENIAL FLAME OF CHARITY IN THE HEART.**

*Washington Irving*

**IF YOU HAVEN'T GOT ANY CHARITY IN YOUR HEART, YOU HAVE THE WORST KIND OF HEART TROUBLE.**

*Bob Hope*

**REMEMBER, IF CHRISTMAS ISN'T FOUND IN YOUR HEART, YOU WON'T FIND IT UNDER A TREE.**

*Charlotte Carpenter*

**I WISH WE COULD PUT UP SOME OF THE CHRISTMAS SPIRIT IN JARS AND OPEN A JAR OF IT EVERY MONTH.**

*Harlan Miller*

**ONE OF THE NICE THINGS ABOUT CHRISTMAS IS THAT YOU CAN MAKE PEOPLE FORGET THE PAST WITH A PRESENT.**

*Anon*

**CHRISTMAS GIFT SUGGESTIONS: TO YOUR ENEMY, FORGIVENESS. TO AN OPPONENT, TOLERANCE. TO A FRIEND, YOUR HEART. TO A CUSTOMER, SERVICE. TO ALL, CHARITY. TO EVERY CHILD, A GOOD EXAMPLE. TO YOURSELF, RESPECT.**

*Oren Arnold*

**UNLESS WE MAKE CHRISTMAS AN OCCASION TO SHARE OUR BLESSINGS, ALL THE SNOW IN ALASKA WON'T MAKE IT 'WHITE'.**

*Bing Crosby*

**CHRISTMAS IS NOT A TIME NOR A SEASON, BUT A STATE OF MIND. TO CHERISH PEACE AND GOODWILL, TO BE PLENTEOUS IN MERCY, IS TO HAVE THE REAL SPIRIT OF CHRISTMAS.**

*Calvin Coolidge*

# BAH HUMBUG

**CHRISTMAS IS A TIME WHEN YOU GET HOMESICK — EVEN WHEN YOU'RE HOME.**

*Carol Nelson*

**'A MERRY CHRISTMAS, UNCLE! GOD SAVE YOU!' CRIED A CHEERFUL VOICE. 'BAH' SAID SCROOGE. 'HUMBUG!'**

*Charles Dickens*

**A SEVERED FOOT IS THE PERFECT STOCKING STUFFER.**

*Mitch Hedberg*

# MERRY CHRISTMAS, NEARLY EVERYBODY!

*Ogden Nash*

# BLAST THIS CHRISTMAS MUSIC. IT'S JOYFUL AND TRIUMPHANT.

*Grinch (Jim Carrey) in 'How the Grinch Stole Christmas'*

**BAH! HOW HOLLOW IT ALL IS! ALWAYS ON CHRISTMAS, THOUGH, I FEEL MY OWN HEART SOFTEN—TOWARD THE LATE JUDAS ISCARIOT.**

*Ambrose Bierce*

# COMFORT AND JOY

**A LOVELY THING ABOUT CHRISTMAS IS THAT IT'S COMPULSORY, LIKE A THUNDERSTORM, AND WE ALL GO THROUGH IT TOGETHER.**

*Garrison Keillor*

**AT CHRISTMAS PLAY AND MAKE GOOD CHEER, FOR CHRISTMAS COMES BUT ONCE A YEAR.**

*Thomas Tusser*

**GIFTS OF TIME AND LOVE ARE SURELY THE BASIC INGREDIENTS OF A TRULY MERRY CHRISTMAS.**

*Peg Bracken*

**CHRISTMAS IS A BRIDGE. WE NEED BRIDGES AS THE RIVER OF TIME FLOWS PAST. TODAY'S CHRISTMAS SHOULD MEAN CREATING HAPPY HOURS FOR TOMORROW AND RELIVING THOSE OF YESTERDAY.**

*Gladys Taber*

# RELIGION

**HOW MANY OBSERVE CHRIST'S BIRTHDAY! HOW FEW, HIS PRECEPTS! O! 'TIS EASIER TO KEEP HOLIDAYS THAN COMMANDMENTS.**

*Benjamin Franklin*

**WHEN WE WERE CHILDREN WE WERE GRATEFUL TO THOSE WHO FILLED OUR STOCKINGS AT CHRISTMAS TIME. WHY ARE WE NOT GRATEFUL TO GOD FOR FILLING OUR STOCKINGS WITH LEGS?**

*G K Chesterton*

**THIS IS THE MESSAGE OF CHRISTMAS: WE ARE NEVER ALONE.**

*Taylor Caldwell*

**THE CHRISTMAS TREE HAS TAKEN THE PLACE OF THE ALTAR IN TOO MUCH OF OUR MODERN CHRISTMAS OBSERVANCE.**

*Anon*

**CHRISTMAS WAVES A MAGIC WAND OVER THIS WORLD, AND BEHOLD, EVERYTHING IS SOFTER AND MORE BEAUTIFUL.**

*Norman Vincent Peale*

**ROSES ARE REDDISH
VIOLETS ARE BLUISH
IF IT WEREN'T FOR
CHRISTMAS
WE'D ALL BE JEWISH.**

*Benny Hill*

# SPIRIT OF CHRISTMAS

**NEXT TO A CIRCUS THERE AIN'T NOTHING THAT PACKS UP AND TEARS OUT FASTER THAN THE CHRISTMAS SPIRIT.**

*Kin Hubbard*

**CHRISTMAS IS NOT AS MUCH ABOUT OPENING OUR PRESENTS AS OPENING OUR HEARTS.**

*Janice Maeditere*

**THERE IS NO IDEAL CHRISTMAS; ONLY THE ONE CHRISTMAS YOU DECIDE TO MAKE AS A REFLECTION OF YOUR VALUES, DESIRES, AFFECTIONS, TRADITIONS.**

*Bill McKibben*

**MAY WE NOT 'SPEND' CHRISTMAS OR 'OBSERVE' CHRISTMAS, BUT RATHER 'KEEP' IT.**

*Peter Marshall*

**AT CHRISTMAS I NO MORE DESIRE A ROSE, THAN WISH A SNOW IN MAY'S NEW-FANGLED SHOWS; BUT LIKE OF EACH THING THAT IN SEASON GROWS.**

*William Shakespeare*

**THERE MUST BE SOMETHING GHOSTLY IN THE AIR OF CHRISTMAS— SOMETHING ABOUT THE CLOSE, MUGGY ATMOSPHERE THAT DRAWS UP THE GHOSTS, LIKE THE DAMPNESS OF THE SUMMER RAINS BRINGS OUT THE FROGS AND SNAILS.**

*Jerome K Jerome*

# NEW YEAR

**NEW YEAR'S IS A HARMLESS ANNUAL INSTITUTION, OF NO PARTICULAR USE TO ANYBODY SAVE AS A SCAPEGOAT FOR PROMISCUOUS DRUNKS, AND FRIENDLY CALLS AND HUMBUG RESOLUTIONS.**

*Mark Twain*

**MAY ALL YOUR TROUBLES LAST AS LONG AS YOUR NEW YEAR'S RESOLUTIONS.**

*Joey Adams*

**GOOD RESOLUTIONS ARE SIMPLY CHECKS THAT MEN DRAW ON A BANK WHERE THEY HAVE NO ACCOUNT.**

*Oscar Wilde*

**NEW YEAR'S EVE, WHERE AULD ACQUAINTANCE BE FORGOT. UNLESS, OF COURSE, THOSE TESTS COME BACK POSITIVE.**

*Jay Leno*

**NEW YEAR'S DAY... NOW IS THE ACCEPTED TIME TO MAKE YOUR REGULAR ANNUAL GOOD RESOLUTIONS. NEXT WEEK YOU CAN BEGIN PAVING HELL WITH THEM AS USUAL.**

*Mark Twain*

**YOUTH IS WHEN YOU'RE ALLOWED TO STAY UP LATE ON NEW YEAR'S EVE. MIDDLE AGE IS WHEN YOU'RE FORCED TO.**

*Bill Vaughan*

**RING OUT THE OLD, RING IN THE NEW, RING, HAPPY BELLS, ACROSS THE SNOW: THE YEAR IS GOING, LET HIM GO; RING OUT THE FALSE, RING IN THE TRUE.**

*Alfred Lord Tennyson*

# MORE HELP IS AT HAND...